SAINT PATRICK

Patron Saint of Ireland

Lois Rock
Illustrated by Finola Stack

LION
CHILDREN'S

Who Was Patrick?

Patrick was a real person in Irish history, and quite a lot is known about him.

He lived about 1,500 years ago, at a time when the Romans had an empire that spread far beyond the city of Rome, as far as parts of the British Isles. Christianity was by that time the official religion of the empire. In Ireland, which

This stained-glass picture shows Patrick dressed as a bishop.

4

was just outside the empire, some people had heard about the message of Jesus Christ and lived as Christians. Many others still clung to the old religion and were fearful of dark forces in the world around them.

Patrick had many adventures as a young man and later became a missionary to the Irish. He set up many churches and helped people understand how to live as followers of Jesus.

He wrote an account of his own life, the *Confession*, in which he thanked God for helping him in everything.

After Patrick died, many more tales and legends were told about him, claiming that he did some amazing things. Although these legends may not be true, they help show what an important person he was to the Irish people and to the Christian faith.

Patrick: Missionary to the Irish

ALPURNIUS AND CONCHESSA were delighted. They had a new baby son. 'We will give him all the good things that money can buy,' they said.

So the little boy grew up in their lovely villa in the countryside. When he was sixteen and looking forward to becoming a scholar, disaster struck. Raiders from across the sea came to plunder the land. They found the lad and seized him. 'We can sell him as a slave,' they shouted.

The raiders flung Patrick

6

into a boat and took him back with them to Ireland. At the slave market, a chieftain named Milchu was looking for someone to take care of his flocks of sheep. He was a powerful man, and also a druid – a priest of the ancient religion of Ireland. No one dared cross a druid, for they alone understood the dark forces that left everyone else afraid.

'I need someone strong and healthy,' he said to the traders. 'It's a hard life being a shepherd. I need someone who will survive days and nights out on the hills, even when the cold rain blows in from the great, grey ocean.'

So he chose Patrick.

The young slave was set to work on the windswept hills. From fellow workers he heard whispers of the dark forces in which the Irish believed. He heard of the mysterious rituals of the druids. He listened, fearful, as tales were told of wars between chieftains, of fighting and bloodshed.

As a boy, Patrick had not been at all interested in anything to do with God. Now, far from home and afraid, his faith grew. A hundred times a day, he prayed to God. Even in the freezing winter, he liked to get up before sunrise to begin his prayers.

The years passed. One night, in a dream, he believed he heard God telling him that he would soon be returning to his homeland. 'And then I shall be safe again,' he said to himself. 'I will dare: I will make the journey, whatever perils I meet along the way.'

And so he did. Not long after this dream, he made his escape, boarded a ship and eventually came to a safe landing. Now, all he wanted to do was to live for God. He studied hard to become a leader in the church.

Years went by. Then Patrick had a strange dream, and in his dream he felt sure he heard the Irish people calling him. 'Come and live among us again,' they cried.

So Patrick went back to the land where he had been a slave. He was a good missionary: he remembered that he, too, had once found it hard to believe in God, and he was clever at using simple words to help people understand.

He remembered that he, too, had done wrong things in his life, so he was ready to welcome people who were wrongdoers.

Crowds came to find out what Patrick was doing. 'What you say rings true,' said many. 'We want to live as followers of Jesus.' Patrick baptized them as a sign of their new faith.

Patrick faced many dangers as well. The local chieftains were suspicious of him and even tried to

kill him, but Patrick was confident. 'God is helping me,' he said. 'I trust in God to protect me.'

It seems that God was faithful to Patrick. As the years went by, Patrick drove out the old religion and all its fears. Thousands became Christians, meeting in little churches all over Ireland and giving their whole lives to serve God through prayer and good deeds.

The Legend of the Easter Fire

The greatest of the Irish chieftains, King Leoghaire, had sent his messengers far and wide. All the chieftains were to meet at Tara for a great feast. There was also a command issued to all the land: on the night of the feast, all fires were to be put out. They must only be relit when a beacon fire blazed out from the king's own stronghold.

Patrick heard the news, and knew what he must do.

He travelled with his companions to

Tara and set up camp within sight of the king's stronghold. 'Tomorrow is Easter Day,' he told his friends. 'We will light our fire just before the dawn, in honour of the resurrection of our Lord Jesus.'

The king was furious when he saw Patrick's fire. His druids gathered round. 'Kill the one who has disobeyed,' they warned him, 'or his fire will burn more brightly than yours in this land.'

The king sent fighting men to capture Patrick and his followers… but when they drew near, they saw no one, only a small herd of deer trotting peaceably away through the woods.

13

The Legend of the Shamrock

One day, Patrick was talking to the people about the One True God, who was greater than all the gods of the old religion.

'If there is one God, then who is Jesus?' came the question. 'And when you baptize, why do you baptize people in the name of God the Father, God the Son and God the Holy Spirit?'

Patrick thought for a moment. Then he stooped down to the ground and plucked a tiny stem from the plant at his feet. It was a shamrock, one of the first plants to unfold in spring.

'Look,' he said. This shamrock leaf is like three green hearts; but it is not three leaves, for they all come from the one stem. In the same way, God is One, but we know God's love in three ways:

the love of God the Father, who made the world;
the love of God the Son: Jesus, who came to save us;
the love of God the Holy Spirit, who enables us to live as God's friends.

'God,' said Patrick, 'is three-in-one, three in unity: Trinity.'
He said this prayer:

I bind to myself today
the name of Trinity:
the strength of Father, Spirit, Son:
the three in unity.

The Legend of the Snakes

There is a legend that Patrick drove the snakes out of Ireland; but scientists say that there have never been snakes in Ireland!

Most people agree that the legend has another meaning. The snake has often been used as a picture of everything that is evil because of the story of the Garden of Eden in the Bible. What Patrick did was drive evil out of Ireland as he spread the Christian message of peace and goodness.

The Legend of the Cross

The shape of the Celtic cross is often linked to Patrick and his teaching. It is a cross with the shape of the sun around it. In the old religion of Ireland, people worshipped the sun as a god. Patrick taught that Jesus, who died on a cross of wood, was the true God, the true sun. In this way he used ancient Irish symbols to explain more about Christianity.

Saint Patrick's Breastplate

It is said that Patrick armed himself before doing battle with the forces of the old religion. His armour was the armour of God – a prayer. Opposite is a part of it. In the prayer, he claims that all the things in the world around, which the druids believed they could command, belong to heaven, and he asks for God's protection.

It is not certain that Patrick himself wrote this prayer; but it does seem to be inspired by his life and deeds.

I bind to myself today
the power of heaven:
the power of bright sun
and gleaming moon;
the power of burning fire
and flashing lightning;
the power of rushing wind
and swelling sea;
the power of deep earth
and solid rock.

I bind to myself today
God's power to guide me,
God's might to uphold me,
God's wisdom to teach me,
God's eye to watch over me,
God's ear to hear me;

God's word to guide
my speaking,
God's hand to guide
my doing,
God's way to guide
my walking,
God's shield to guard
my being;

God's angels to keep
me from every snare
and every danger.

Saint Patrick's Day

Saint Patrick's Day is on 17 March, the day Patrick is believed to have died. It is a national holiday in Ireland. It falls in the Christian season of Lent, which is a time of fasting and frugality; but in Ireland even the most religious of people who go to church in the morning enjoy an un-Lenten celebration for the rest of the day!

Traditional Irish dancing depends on fast and nimble footwork.

As well as remembering Saint Patrick, it is a time to celebrate all things Irish. On this day there are parades, concerts, outdoor theatre shows and fireworks.

Traditional Irish music is often heard – lively dance tunes and mournful laments. Instruments played include the harp, fiddle, tin whistle, a hand drum called the bodhrán, and bagpipes known as the uilleann pipes.

Saint Patrick's Day was celebrated in America from the early days of British settlement there. An Irish regiment established a parade in New York. Then, about 150 years ago, there was famine in Ireland when the potato crop failed. Many Irish people went to America to find a better living. They were delighted to find Saint Patrick's Day celebrations had already arrived. Over the years, the celebrations have become more enthusiastic and include many Americans who do not have an Irish background.

Index

Text by Lois Rock
Illustrations copyright © 2005 Finola Stack
This edition copyright © 2005 Lion Hudson

The moral rights of the author and illustrator
have been asserted

A Lion Children's Book
an imprint of
Lion Hudson plc
Mayfield House, 256 Banbury Road,
Oxford OX2 7DH, England
www.lionhudson.com
ISBN 0 7459 4811 1

First edition 2005
10 9 8 7 6 5 4 3 2 1 0

A catalogue record for this book is available
from the British Library

Typeset in 15/20 Revival565 BT
Printed and bound in Singapore

Picture Acknowledgments
Front cover: Sonia Halliday Photographs
Alamy Ltd: p. 20
Sonia Halliday Photographs: p. 4